WHY CHRISTIAN MEN NEED EACH OTHER

WHY CHRISTIAN MEN NEED EACH OTHER

PETE RICHARDSON

Gary J. Oliver, Ph.D., General Editor

MOODY PRESS

CHICAGO

Redwood trees are the giants of the forest. They tower above the earth at heights of over three hundred feet. Unlike most trees, which send their roots to a depth equaling their height, redwoods send their roots outward, intermingling their roots with one another. Together they form a fortified unit, a secure stronghold that allows these giants to withstand high winds.

That is how strength is achieved among men as well, by working together as a unified whole. Men working together brings strength, whether dealing in the workplace, leading families at home, or serving in churches. Unfortunately, individualism among men prevails in the church. In fact, the individual approach has produced a generation of isolated church men.

The individualism among men at church imitates the independence and surface relationships among men in American society. As men, we often find our friendships are as deep as the following conversation between Sam and John.

"Hi, Sam. How are you?"
"Great, John. You?"
"OK. How's work?"
"Busy. Did you get that contract?"
"Yes. I did."
"Great. Hey, good to see you."
"Yeah. You too."
"Take care."
"See you next week."

Sound familiar? Perhaps this is why so many Christian men feel disconnected and isolated. Perhaps you are one of them. Individualism has left men stranded to try "to do the job alone"—a job that is supposed to be done as a team. In his book *The Friendless American Male*, David Smith recounts the story of a man filing an insurance claim for on-the-job injuries. The story illustrates the consequences of ignoring teamwork to go it alone.

Dear Sir,

I am writing in response to your request for more information concerning block 11 on the insurance form, which asks for "cause of injuries," wherein I put "Trying to do the job alone." You said you needed more information so I trust the following will be sufficient.

I am a bricklayer by trade, and on the date of the injuries I was working alone laying brick around the top of a four-story building, when I realized that I had about 500 pounds of bricks left over. Rather than carry the bricks down by hand, I decided to put them into a barrel and lower them by a pulley, which was fastened to the top of the building. I secured the end of the rope at ground level, and went up to the top of the building, and loaded the bricks into the barrel, and swung the barrel out with the bricks in it. I then went down and untied the rope, holding it securely to slow the descent of the barrel.

As you will note in block 6 of the insurance form, I weigh a hundred and forty-five pounds. Due to my shock at being jerked off the ground so swiftly, I lost my presence of mind and forgot to let go of the rope. Between the second and third floors, I met the barrel coming down. This accounts for the bruises and lacerations on my upper body.

Regaining my presence of mind again, I held tightly to the rope and proceeded up the side of the building, not stopping until my right hand was jammed in the pulley. This accounts for the broken thumb. Despite the pain, I retained my presence of mind and held tightly to the rope. At approximately the same time, however, the bottom fell out of the barrel and the bricks fell out on the ground. Devoid of the weight of the bricks, the barrel now weighed about fifty pounds. I again refer you to block 6 and my weight.

As you would guess, I began a rapid descent. In the vicinity of the second floor, I met the barrel coming up. This explains the injuries to my legs and lower body. Slowed only slightly, I continued my descent, landing on the pile of bricks. This accounts for my sprained back and internal injuries.

I am sorry to report, however, that at this point, I lost my presence of mind and let go of the rope, and as you can imagine, the empty barrel crashed down on me. This accounts for my head injuries. I trust this answers your concern. Please know that I am finished "Trying to do the job alone."[1]

We weren't created to live in isolation. But we often act as if we were! Many of us have been beat up as a result, just like the bricklayer. We have tried "to do the job alone." Men, we need each other!

Roadblocks to Ministry

Yet many church leaders report frustration in trying to begin or continue a church-based men's ministry. If we agree that men need one another, why have men's ministries experienced only limited success in the past? The primary reason is that we men are isolated as part of an American culture that teaches men to be tough individualists.

We are isolated and don't know it. We lack friendships that can survive the valleys of life. Researcher George Barna concludes that "Americans are among the loneliest people on earth."[2] Sure, we spend time with other men in the context of work, play, hobbies, or other interests. But such relationships form acquaintances and companions, not friends. Smith notes that "Men find it hard to accept the fact that they need the deep fellowship of other men."[3]

If you desire to begin or energize a men's ministry in your church, keep in mind that men may resist for three reasons. First, men tend to make projects and goals more important than relationships. We men are highly task-oriented, and that emphasis can carry over in the church setting, where men want to know what they will receive from such a ministry. They look to outcomes first and to relationships second.

Second, most men are leery of heart-to-heart relationships. Men don't like being exposed among church friends as being needy and incomplete in their spiritual and emotional lives. "We men fear anything that robs us of our power and control, anything that might make us look less like a man," argues Gary Oliver. "Typically this means we avoid anything that shows lack of courage or our being fearful. To be a coward is to be a wimp, not a man."[4] Consequently, most of us have learned to look good on the outside when we hurt on the inside. However, we need other men, and a men's ministry needs to address those needs.

Third, men lack models. Many men have been reared by fathers who could not and would not communicate. Their fathers were only passing on the mistaken myth of the self-contained man. "It's a cycle of uncertainty that seems endless. Fathers don't know how to deal with sons because their own fathers didn't know how to deal with them."[5] Most of us never saw our dads connect with other men in meaningful, lasting friendships. Thus, we are hesitant to expose ourselves to honest relationships that spring from men's groups.

Yet the call for men to come together finds its origins in Jesus' prayer in John 17:21 that we would "be one" just as He and the Father are one. Christ didn't pray that we would stand strong as rugged individualists. He prayed that we would be networked to each other through our faith in him. Paul compared the body of Christ to the human body, stating that all parts of the body must recognize their connectedness to the rest of the body. In 1 Corinthians 12:26 he wrote, "If one part suffers, every part suffers with it; if one part is honored, every part rejoices with it."

God can form us men into a fortified unit, just like the redwood forests. Our greatest enemy to coming together, however, is our tendency to isolate ourselves. Once church leaders recognize this truth, they can develop programs that connect with Christian men.

Men can come together in many ways in the church, from small accountability groups to larger men's breakfasts and to national conferences. All of these are part of the best mechanism for welding men together: a church-sponsored men's ministry.

The Men's Movement

The idea of starting a men's ministry has not always set well with leaders in the local church. Just five years ago, the common response to such a proposal went something like this: "You can bring men together for an athletic event or for good food. But to consistently gather them for accountability and spiritual growth, for prayer and worship? Forget it!"

Church leaders have good reason to feel this way. Since the 1950s they have increasingly emphasized family-centered programs and events in an attempt to help sustain families in the church. For the most part, women have taken the front seat in this church participation and attention—and men have settled in the back. The unintended result—only 30–40 percent of adults at church on a given Sunday morning are men.[6]

The main reason churches have focused on families and women instead of men has been men's inconsistent support of programs for men. And that is due to their task orientation, fear of heart-to-heart relationships, and the poor modeling they received from their own fathers, as noted above. Consequently, stories of failed men's ministries abound.

Yet change is underway. Men are beginning to see the need for close fellowship with other men, and innovative ministries are helping men deal with their fears and see the benefits of unifying with other men. Consider the following two examples. At Campus Baptist Church in Fresno, Calif., men's small groups focus on relationships and accountability. Lee Stallings, administrative pastor, says candidly, "Our men are theologically pure but relationally bankrupt." But they are becoming more involved because "men are now willing to talk," Stallings reports. As a result of the groups and special men's events and meetings, many more men are volunteering for leadership roles in the church.

In West Columbia, South Carolina, almost half the men at Northside Baptist Church are participating in the men's ministry, a mix of men's special events, men's congregational gatherings, and a choice of three kinds of small groups for men—spiritual growth, encouragement, or discipleship (each group requiring a greater degree of commitment).

The ministry at Northside has grown gradually during the past five years, and Associate Pastor Ross Robinson acknowledges leaders must be aware of men's busy schedules and task orientation. "The first few years [of men's ministry] are tough. Men don't see the value of men's ministry at first. Their schedules are already full." Robinson believes selection and training of leaders is crucial for a successful men's ministry. He advises leaders who are beginning a men's ministry to start with a few men. Now 50 percent of the men are active.

LINKING WITH OTHER MEN

The experiences and research at Promise Keepers, a national ministry to develop spiritual commitments among men, clearly indicate men are seeking spiritual growth and accountability through linking with other men. In the past three years, we have watched the call for men to meet together annually for worship, prayer, and teaching on what it means to be men of God draw an increasingly powerful response.

In July 1991, 4,200 men assembled in the Events Center at the University of Colorado; in July 1992, 22,000 men converged at the university's football stadium, Folsom Field. In 1993 more than 50,000 men assembled in the stadium—not for a football game featuring the university's successful Buffalo athletes, but to hear the challenge to become men of integrity, men of God.

The interest among men to gather with other men and learn about God has resulted in the Promise Keepers organization offering six regional conferences beginning in 1994. Conference organizers project that more than 120,000 men will attend at the six locations.

Promise Keepers is only one manifestation of the interest among men to draw close to God, become spiritual leaders in their homes, and be accountable to other men. Many pastors, Christian leaders, and wives report an increasing spiritual hunger among their men. As research director at Promise Keepers, I have come to an obvious conclusion: God is stirring the hearts of men in our nation in a unique and exciting way!

"I had never been able to sustain a close relationship with God for any length of time before," says Jeff Sable of Bethany, Oklahoma. "Now, I thank a small group of guys who support and encourage me and keep me accountable, as I do them." We hear reports of men gathering at different times during the day to pray and study God's Word. Many are embracing their leadership responsibilities in their families, churches, and communities. Others are experiencing the benefits of encouragement and support in men's small groups, rather than facing life in isolation. Men are forging ahead in conviction, integrity, and action. Here's just a sampling of what they are saying.

Larry Alexander of Colorado found that he benefited from having relationships with older men. "These men are ten to twenty years older than me. What impresses me the most about them is that they are real. And they're real because they have gone through the fire—they've been tested and their faith has been strengthened because they passed the tests. Their faith is not just in their heads; it's not a game to them. It's not like they are still trying to be Christians; they *are* Christians. I want to be like that."

There is great potential when men unite based upon what they have in common. Imagine what would happen if the men in your church began to unite together, based simply on their faith in Jesus Christ. What would happen if they met weekly to pray for each other, their families, your pastor, church, and community? What would happen if they began to challenge each other with the truth of God's Word? What would happen if they loyally defended each other's reputations? What would happen if they banded together when a brother fell, or did all that they could to help each man increase in his faith in God?

Men gathering together also can have a positive impact on marriages and families. A network of Christian brothers who accept, encourage, and exhort us will clearly benefit our families. They can remind us to pursue the eternal issues that affect our families and marriages as aggressively as we pursue the temporal. Imagine what could happen to our communities and our nation if hundreds of thousands—even millions—of Christian men stood for truth, integrity, and godliness?

This may sound like a pipe dream to you. But in significant ways it is already happening. Consider the men at a Bible Community church in Colorado who agreed to be accountable in a men's ministry. Several church leaders organized the ministry, called "The Pace Setters," with the motto "A Man's Man Is a Godly Man." The Pace Setters define their purpose as "Helping men set the pace in their families, in our church, and in our community." They believe that if they help each other grow in their faith and in their walk with God, then they will set the pace for the next generation.

During its two years the ministry has shown rapid growth, both in numbers and spiritual maturity. After one year, one hundred men from Bible Community attended the 1993 Promise Keepers national conference. Now almost half of the 180 men at Community meet once a month for a Saturday morning breakfast, a fifteen minute devotional, and a time to articulate personal needs and then pray with other men. To reach out to men in their community, they have organized special events: father-son fish fries, wild-game cookouts, athletic events, and so forth.

THE THREE P'S

At Bible Community twenty small groups of four or five men each meet in "squads." The squads assemble weekly to focus on the three "Ps":

prayer, the *pages* of Scripture, and understanding each other's *pain*.

Jim tells a story about how his squad is beginning to connect on the tough issues. His friend Dave had suffered a business failure but seemed to be accepting it well. He found a new job and was regularly attending the weekly squad meetings. One week, the group watched a video on how a man can strengthen his marriage. Jim recalled how Dave seemed encouraged in his marriage to Beth.

The next night, Jim answered the phone to hear a quivering, crying voice—Dave's wife, Beth. "Jim," she began, "Dave just came home and told me that he wants a divorce. He said that he just doesn't love me anymore and that I'd be better off without him."

Jim contacted Dave the following day at work, and Dave reluctantly agreed to meet with him and talk about his problems. According to Jim, Dave needed professional help to sort through his feelings. Dave later agreed to see a Christian counselor, and his squad of Pace Setters paid for the counseling. After the counselor heard what the group was doing, he lowered the already low fees another 40 percent. Now it looks like Dave and Beth's marriage is going to make it.

Jim commented, "We are beginning to connect. It's harder to isolate yourself when you have brothers who really care about you!" These men had shared enough, felt enough, and trusted enough that they could not stand by and watch the marriage of their brother crash. They sounded a 911 emergency alarm and went after him. Jim continued, "God is using us to spur each other on as men of God. Our wives are the first to say how much we have changed for the good."

Are you connected with other Christian men? Do you have a 911 emergency team at your disposal? Do you have a sounding board? Who do you turn to if you need to talk? A great resource exists in the men in your church, but they must be connected. The most effective way is to meet together regularly in order to encourage each other in your faith.

If such a group of caring men does not exist in your church, you can take steps to become connected with your brothers in Christ through vital, genuine relationships. With the right network of men you can help develop an effective ministry to the men in your church. Together such a group can network with other Christian men in your community and make a difference.

Helping Men Connect

Last year, Promise Keepers conducted a men's ministry survey, interviewing pastors and laymen in churches that had some form of men's ministry—churches of various sizes, geographic locations, denominational and ethnic backgrounds. We asked them twenty-eight questions in personal and telephone interviews. The insights discussed in this section are based on this research.[7]

Our findings revealed that effective men's ministries strategically organize different types of gatherings, types that complement each other as a whole. We identified five distinct types of men's gatherings: conferences, special events, equipping seminars, congregational gatherings, and small groups. The funnel model in Figure 1 illustrates how they fit together.

Just as a real funnel provides the parameters for directing a liquid into a container, this funnel illustrates the progression, beginning at the top, of two critical components of men's ministry: (1) biblical information and (2) relational commitment.

The left arrow represents the biblical information given in a particular gathering; the right arrow represents the level of relational commitment required for a particular gathering.

Clearly both must exist for men to be willing to make and to keep promises. As we move down the funnel to more intimate gatherings, those meetings impart a greater amount of biblical information and require a greater degree of relational commitment. A small group, for example, is more focused on implementing biblical directives and requires greater relational commitment from a man than a special event, such as a father-son campout.

Because maturity is a process, it is necessary to provide a variety of opportunities for men to grow in their relationships with Christ and each other. That is why the most important guideline to remember when you attempt to gather men in your church is this: *Provide a variety of entry points into the men's ministry.* Follow this guideline and you'll make it easy for men to get involved, and you will eliminate many unnecessary setbacks and frustrations. Though the arrows in Figure 1 show men entering through men's conferences and men's special events, in truth the arrows can point to all five entry points.

Our research shows, however, that effective men's ministries have a nonthreatening "front door." The primary entry point is an easy-access special event or conference. The other entry points act as secondary entrances. Yet each is important. Beginning at the top of the funnel model, let's consider the entry points one at a time.

MEN'S CONFERENCES

These are city, state, and national parachurch or interchurch gatherings, such as the Promise Keepers' National Men's Conferences. These gatherings act as catalysts to motivate men to become godly and to jump-start men's ministries. Many men return from these conferences having made life-changing commitments to Jesus Christ, their families, friends, and churches.

In Chicago, men have gathered the past three years for the Moody Men's Conference. In 1994, more than 1,400 heard dynamic speakers, such as Tony Evans and Joe Stowell, challenge them to godliness.

In Grand Rapids, Michigan, Men's Life offers seminars and conferences to local churches, as well as co-ordinates men's small group Bible studies nationwide to evangelize men and assimilate them into churches.

Those who attend men's conferences testify to the impact. "The Moody Men's Conference has challenged me to keep my thoughts fixed on what will glorify God rather than anything else," said Paul of Valparaiso, Indiana.

Julie, from British Columbia, said, "The Promise Keepers' weekend was truly a blessing, not only for my husband, but for me as well. I received the full benefit of an excited, spiritually refreshed husband who was (and still is) determined to be a 'real man'—one who is a 'promise keeper.'"

Louis of Levelland, Texas, called his experience at a national men's conference (Promise Keepers) "the best thing that has ever happened in my life (second to Jesus and me!)." Louis said he was changed and now has a vision for other men. He has since met with the pastor of his church and has begun a men's ministry. "The men meet Thursday night every week; and the changes are awesome! The wives will be the first to tell you how things have improved in every way in the home, spiritually and physically."

When the local church links catalytic men's conferences to its men's ministry, they strengthen their mission, families, and leadership. When these men return from a national conference, having gathered with thousands of men from around the country to honor Jesus Christ, it is a prime opportunity for a pastor and church to capitalize on this spiritual momentum. They can immediately offer entry points into men's small groups and other activities.

MEN'S SPECIAL EVENTS

Activity-oriented events offer opportunities for men to become acquainted with each other through nonthreatening entry points. Successful special events for men have included steak fries with an afternoon of softball or basketball, bowling leagues, hunting adventures, chili cook-offs with special recognition of the winners, father-daughter formal banquets, and father-son campouts.

For many, these activities are the first points of contact with other men, providing opportunities to communicate on the level of "what they do" and to interact with one another based upon what they have in common—hobbies, politics, music, and sports. At this level, a man can begin to alter his posture in the church from spectator to participant.

Such gatherings can become important first steps for men who have few or no relationships with other men. They need nonthreatening entry points where others will not ask them to take relational risks for which they are not prepared (such as breaking into a small group to share personal struggles). Without these low-risk gatherings, most men on the periphery of church life or in the community will not sacrifice their time to attend.

The keys to a successful special event is that it be nonthreatening and activity-focused. It is the front door into the men's ministry. In order for this gathering to be effective, it must offer the opportunity for a man to participate in the other categories of men's gatherings, such as equipping seminars and small groups. However, if this is the only ministry to men that the church offers, the danger exists of it becoming a men's social club with no avenues to challenge men spiritually and relationally.

God calls all men to grow as leaders in some manner, and equipping seminars offer them the opportunity to invest in their personal growth and leadership skills. The National Center for Fathering, for example, offers an excellent seminar on "The Seven Secrets of Effective Fathers," and Promise Keepers offers a training seminar for men's ministry leadership.[8] Local churches can host these seminars by contacting the organizations directly.

If a man has initiated friendships through special events, then the odds of him accepting an invitation to attend a teaching seminar increase greatly. In this case he would have friends to encourage his attendance by riding together and enjoying and discussing the seminar together.

MEN'S CONGREGATIONAL GATHERINGS

At men's congregational gatherings, all the men in the church are invited to gather for teaching, fellowship, and prayer. The two most common examples are a men's retreat and a monthly men's breakfast. These gatherings can challenge a man to implement Christlike action into his relationships and may provide greater opportunities to interact on the level of who he is and not just on what he does.

Because these gatherings impart more biblical information and require a greater degree of interaction among men, they are oriented less to aiding the non-Christian man and more to nurturing the Christian man. The information directly challenges men to pursue godliness, with the help and accountability of their Christian brothers.

Generally, a small group is a regular gathering of two to twelve men. Of all the levels on the funnel, this one possesses the greatest potential for spiritual growth. In the context of small groups, men can study Scripture and express their hopes and fears. The men experience the challenges of self-disclosure and committing themselves to mutual support and encouragement. Here a man interacts beyond the level of what he does and who he is to a deeper level—"what he struggles with" and "how he is going to succeed."

Many small groups ask for a level of accountability, where a man is accountable for his actions to others in the group. Bob Beltz's booklet in this series, *Accountability Among Men*, addresses the importance of having these kinds of relationships

and how you can become accountable with other men.

By dedicating himself to grow
spiritually along with other men, a
man begins to resolve any inherent
problems resulting from isolation in
his life. He has chosen to become a
member of a team. Standing with others, each individual succeeds in his
call to honor Jesus Christ and in the
mission of the church.

Outreach

When a man makes and keeps
his promises to Jesus Christ, his integrity has a positive ripple effect in
the lives of others. Because of God's
work in his life, he becomes an am-
bassador for bringing more men into
the funnel process of men's ministry.
He becomes a living model of a
"promise keeper" to his family,
church, friends, and community. He
joins a generation of "men of action,"
men who are mutually committed to
making a difference.

STEVE'S BUSY SCHEDULE

Steve's story illustrates how the
various levels on the funnel model fit
together and provide avenues for
joining Christian men together
through significant relationships.

One Friday evening Steve loaded
his backpack and placed it near the

front door. He was going away with "the boys"—the men in his small group—for a weekend in the mountains. When his friends arrived to pick Steve up at his house, they enthusiastically greeted him with low-fives and half-hugs. He kissed his wife and kids good-bye and headed to the waiting van.

Steve needed time to relax and recreate with his friends. He had been extremely busy lately and emotionally tired. Often he arrived home from work with little energy to give to his three children. He hadn't planned to go on this trip, but his wife encouraged him. Plus, when he found out that a great fishing river was near the cabin, his decision was made.

He had met Doug, Sam, and Tom ten months earlier at his church. Doug introduced himself to Steve that first Sunday and invited him to come to a Saturday morning men's breakfast. Since Steve expressed interest, Doug offered to pick him up the next Saturday. Steve went and felt immediately welcome at the breakfast. It was early enough that it ended by 8:30 A.M., so he didn't sacrifice his day with the family. He met Sam, Tom, and others that morning, heard a fifteen-minute inspiring message from the pastor, and prayed with two men sitting next to him. He was refreshed by being in the presence of men who were friendly, real, fun, but serious about their faith in God.

In the following months, Steve took his son Jesse on a father-son campout that the men's ministry had planned. That was a special time for his relationship with Jesse. The dads cooked, hiked, fished, and boated with their sons. In the evenings they sat around the fire, sang, told jokes, and talked about what really matters in life. Steve was beginning to develop friendships with other men in his church simply by being with them in nonthreatening circumstances.

It was during the camping trip that Doug invited Steve to join him, Sam, and Tom for a Wednesday morning weekly breakfast. They gathered for prayer, support, and encouragement. The idea intrigued Steve, especially because he knew these men already and felt like he would enjoy spending more time with them. Each week this small group of men talked about a passage from the Bible, shared prayer requests and praises, and prayed for each other.

This small group had become a significant time for Steve. He had had good friends when he was in high school and college. Sports and other interests brought them together. They had since all gone their separate ways, and he hadn't had close friends since then. He had felt a need for more depth to his relationships with other Christian men.

He had children now and was focused on his family and job. He loved his family deeply. Others called him a great husband and dad. But he felt isolated when it came to having friends who really knew him. "My dad never modeled real openness and expressiveness about his feelings," Steve says. "So I had fears even though I wanted guys to know me through trusting friendships. I wanted to connect, really connect with a band of other men."

Steve wanted to be a man of God but felt that he needed the insight, encouragement, and wisdom of his brothers. He now had hope. Perhaps the friendships being forged with the men at his church were what he longed for.

AT THE CABIN

The men arrived at the cabin after stopping for dinner. They settled in, talked about sports and politics in front of the living room fire. Steve was at ease. He reflected on the fact that his faith in God had brought him together with these men. He was feeling comfortable with these guys.

Doug asked Steve how work was going, and Steve talked honestly about the stresses of time-line pressures. Then Tom admitted that he had something to say that he had not talked about before. Steve could tell that this was hard for him. They put their study booklets down to listen.

"I need to talk to you guys about something that I've never shared with anyone else," Tom said. "I heard someone say once that all men have weak spots in one of three areas: girls, gold, or glory. I have been driven in the area of pursuing wealth and accumulating things, in the area of 'gold.' Since I work in an environment where men will do anything for bonuses, I'm tempted constantly to do the same thing. It could potentially destroy my family. I really need your prayer and support."

Saying this was risky for Tom. Steve could tell that he felt alone on this one. But Tom's vulnerability led to a three-hour discussion on how men struggle in the areas of "girls, gold, and glory," and how they could hold one another accountable in a critical, vulnerable area of their lives.

Steve went to bed that night with a lot going through his mind. Tom had taken a risk to be vulnerable. He had opened the door to his heart. His risk allowed the rest of the men to open up. His willingness to let them into his heart, his struggles, his pain, allowed them to connect with each other.

But it didn't happen in one weekend.

They had been meeting faithfully every Wednesday morning for the past fourteen months. Over breakfast they had studied the Bible and shared weekly prayer requests, and they had spent time with one another's families. It had taken time. As Steve thought back over that time and his busy schedule, he figured, *Hey, it's worth it. We've begun to get real with each other and to talk about deep issues face to face. And I'm learning that I'm not alone in my journey as a man.*

The men in Steve's group were beginning to connect because of their desire to be men of God and because of their willingness to spend time together with one unified purpose—to learn about themselves and grow through study of God's Word.

Steve's story illustrates how he was drawn into relationships with other Christian men through a variety of men's gatherings: Saturday breakfasts, campouts, and small groups. The combination of these gatherings helped facilitate the building of his relationships with three other men. When he first attended the church, he wasn't ready to join a small group. But after he began to relate to some of the men, he was ready.

There are some important guidelines from this story we can apply to any ministry among men. If you are interested in beginning or advancing a men's ministry in your church, consider these principles for effective ministry among men.

Four Principles for Men's Ministry

PRINCIPLE #1: VARIETY OF ENTRY POINTS

We're repeating something mentioned earlier, but it is important enough to state again. Not all men are ready to enter into a men's small group. Many men need a less threatening context to get to know each other before they are willing to commit themselves to accountable relationships.

I remember meeting with a group of elders and their pastor to talk about their struggling men's ministry. They had 450 men in their church, and only nine were participating in their men's ministry. I learned that their men's ministry required a high degree of commitment from the start, six to eight weeks of intense Bible study in a small group. We talked about integrating some less threatening special events, such as monthly breakfasts and father-son activities, to draw men into relationship with each other. This simple principle helped them brainstorm all kinds of creative ideas. Each man then took responsibility for one level on the funnel and planned the next year. They are now gathering almost 30 percent of the men in their church on a regular basis.

PRINCIPLE #2: A FOCUS ON
RELATIONSHIPS, NOT PROGRAMS

The principle of relationship clearly guides all effective men's ministries. In general, men do not easily talk about their faith, relationships, and feelings. That's what prompted Baptist pastor Lee Stallings to say earlier (page 12) that his men were theologically pure, but relationally bankrupt." Consequently, the goal of his men's ministry is simply "to encourage men to talk."

One church in Philadelphia organizes an annual men's retreat near a golf course. The men show up on Thursday evening and golf all day Friday before they gather for teaching and small group interaction on Friday night and Saturday. The pastor told us, "If you get the men on turf where they want to talk, they'll talk."

Do not build a men's ministry on programming; rather, focus on facilitating relationship. Make it part of the lifestyle of the church, not just another program to promote.

PRINCIPLE #3: CLEAR GOALS

Howard Hendricks has said, "Aim at nothing, and you will hit it every time." Foundational to your men's ministry is its purpose statement. It is the "North Star," the directional that keeps you on target. It must state who you are and what you are committed to do.

Effective men's ministries have clear goals that are consistently articulated to men. That may be a large part of the success of the Bible Community church mentioned earlier; they had a name, motto, and purpose statement for their ministry. As the Pace Setters, their motto was A Man's Man Is a Godly Man; and their purpose statement declared, "Helping men set the pace in their families, in our church, and in our community." Such goals, when biblically grounded, when applicable to men, and when clearly and consistently articulated, help men take ownership of the men's ministry.

PRINCIPLE #4: A CORE GROUP OF MEN

A majority of the churches that we interviewed (57 percent) started their men's ministry with a group of laymen committed to pray with other men for the men in their church, with a mutual desire to disciple men in issues of conviction, integrity, and action. A pastor's commitment to this core group more likely assures the incorporation of the church's mission into the foundation and philosophy of the men's ministry.

As a pastor invests himself in these men, spiritually and emotionally, he can eventually release them to start their own men's small groups. Often, these men continue to meet regularly for prayer and as a steering council or men's ministry committee.

The core group, then, is the heart of an effective men's ministry—not excluding other men from becoming part of the core group, but certainly providing a foundation of prayer, direction, and leadership for the overall men's ministry.

STAYING ON COURSE

Frank Koch told the following story in *Proceedings*, the magazine of the Naval Institute.

Two battleships assigned to the training squadron had been at sea on maneuvers in heavy weather for several days. I was serving on the lead battleship and was on watch on the bridge as night fell. The visibility was poor with patchy fog, so the captain remained on the bridge keeping an eye on all activities.

Shortly after dark, the lookout on the wing of the bridge reported, "Light, bearing on the starboard bow."

"Is it steady or moving astern?" the captain called out.

Lookout replied, "Steady, captain," which meant we were on a dangerous collision course with that ship.

The captain then called to the signalman, "Signal that ship: We are on a collision course, advise you change course 20 degrees."

Back came the signal, "Advisable for you to change course 20 degrees."

The captain said, "Send, 'I'm a captain, change course 20 degrees.'"

"I'm a seaman second class," came the reply. "You had better change course 20 degrees."

By that time, the captain was furious. He spat out, "Send, 'I'm a battleship. Change course 20 degrees.'"

Back came the flashing light, "I'm a lighthouse."

We changed course.[9]

Principles are like a lighthouse to a ship sailing in thick fog. If heeded, the ministry, like the ship, avoids danger. If not, devastation can follow. Through our survey we discovered that, although each men's ministry was creatively different, certain principles guide all effective men's ministries.

Though they are not steps, the above four principles are based on the experiences of many successful church ministries. So whether your church is just beginning or needs to jump-start an existing ministry, it's wise to listen to the voices of others who have gone before you.

Getting Started

Let me suggest five things that you can do to start gathering the men in your church.

1. TAKE A PROFILE OF YOUR MEN

Effective men's ministries are tailored to fit the interests and needs of a specific group of men. It is important to have insight into your men. Take a few moments and find out the following:

1. How many men are in your church?
2. How many men are currently in small groups?
3. What is the ethnic composition of the men in your church?
4. What is the age range among your men?

5. What are the different interests of these men (hobbies, recreational activities)?
6. How many single and how many married men are in your church?
7. How many fathers are in your church?

Once you have answered these questions, you will have a greater awareness and understanding of where your men are in life. Sensitivity to their cultural backgrounds, their interests, and their responsibilities will help you plan strategically.

2. DEVELOP A CORE GROUP OF MEN

Churches with effective men's ministries are guided by a group of men, laymen and/or pastors who have a collective desire to disciple men in issues of integrity, discipleship, and godliness. When they are actively doing what they are asking other men to do, the foundation is solid. It's important, then, that you establish this core group.

Start by identifying a few men with whom you can meet for prayer, sharing, and encouragement. Write their names on a sheet of paper. Pray about their involvement and for sensitivity in approaching them. Then talk with them one by one and ask them to consider joining you in a time of prayer and encouragement.

3. DEVELOP A PURPOSE STATEMENT

The purpose statement articulates what you intend to accomplish and how you plan to measure the results. For example, the purpose statement of Bible Community's men's ministry is "Helping men set the pace in their families, in our church, and in our community." They measure their effectiveness by how many men participate in their accountability groups, because they believe that if men are accountable they will eventually change.

Now, with your core group develop your own purpose statement. Here are three questions that will help in formulating your statement: (1) What do you want to see happen in the lives of the men in your church? (2) How do you intend to accomplish this? (3) How will you measure the results?

4. PLAN ENTRY POINTS
   INTO YOUR MEN'S MINISTRY

Review the funnel model for men's ministry and make plans to draw men into the various gatherings. An obvious entry point would be a large mens' conference. A regional Promise Keepers conference, for example, could be a springboard for your men's ministry. Before the conference, organize breakfasts and plan to travel together to the event. By attending together, you'll reap long-term benefits. Follow up the conference with a time to share testimonies and later with a men's retreat. Small groups are natural spin-offs of these gatherings.

Whether through small groups or a large national conference, men's ministries can have a major impact on the personal lives of men. "God showed me again the support men can be to each other," says Tim Jenvey of Thomasboro, Ill. Tim attended the 1993 national Promise Keepers conference and learned as much from watching fathers and sons interact as from the conference itself. "God showed me fathers and adult sons close together and sharing their relationship with their God. I've made that a goal for me and my boys."

Christian men need each other. That's why a men's ministry in your church is a worthy goal. Such a ministry can be life-changing for those involved. It can create godly leaders in the church, the family, and the community. It's a goal worth pursuing.

NOTES

1. David Smith, *The Friendless American Male* (Ventura, Calif.: Regal, 1983), 118–19.

2. George Barna, *What Americans Believe* (Ventura, Calif.: Regal, 1991), 74.

3. Smith, 15.

4. Gary Oliver, *Real Men Have Feelings Too* (Chicago: Moody, 1993), 83.

5. James Osterhaus, *Bonds of Iron* (Chicago: Moody, 1994), 41.

6. "The Church's Sexual Demographics," *Leadership Journal*, Winter 1991, 16–20.

7. For an in-depth discussion of the research findings, see Pete Richardson, *Focusing Your Men's Ministry: A Strategy for Lay leaders and Pastors* (Denver: Promise Keepers, 1993) 9–53.

8. The National Center for Fathering is located at 10200 W. 75th St., Shawneee Mission, KS 66204; telephone 913-384-4661; Promise Keepers can be contacted at P.O. Box 18376, Boulder, CO 80308 (303-421-2800). The Moody Men's Conferences are held in Chicago every March and in St. Petersburg, Fla., every October; for information contact Moody Conference Ministries, 820 N. LaSalle Blvd., Chicago, IL 60610 (312-329-4401). Men's Life can be reached at Terry Etter, Men's Life, 2859 Kalamazoo Ave. S.E., Grand Rapids, MI 49560; (800-777-7270).

9. Frank Koch as quoted in Stephen R. Covey, *The 7 Habits of Highly Effective People* (New York: Fireside, 1989), 33.

Promise Keepers is a Christ-centered ministry dedicated to uniting men through vital relationships to become godly influences in their world. Throughout the nation, men are making promises to:

1. Honor Jesus Christ through prayer, worship, and obedience to His Word
2. Practice spiritual, moral, ethical, and sexual purity
3. Build strong marriages and families through love, protection, and biblical values
4. Support the mission of their churches by honoring and praying for their pastors and by actively giving their time and resources
5. Reach beyond racial and denominational barriers to demonstrate the power of biblical unity
6. Influence their world, being obedient to the Great Commandment (love) and the Great Commission (evangelism)
7. Pursue vital relationships with a small group of men, understanding that they need their brothers to help them keep their promises.

Promise Keepers offers the following resources to help a man in this process: conferences, educational services, field ministry, publications, and a resource center. To receive our free Men of Action newsletter featuring updates, resources, and ministry articles, contact Promise Keepers at: P.O. Box 18376, Boulder, CO 80308; 303-421-2800.

At your request, we will send information about becoming a Point Man in your church. A Point Man is the link between his men's ministry and Promise Keepers. He receives additional men's ministry updates and resources.